Pearl the Plott
Tale of a Rescued Dog

CHARLOTTE LEGGE

iUniverse books may be ordered through booksellers or by contacting:

iUniverse
1663 Liberty Drive
Bloomington, IN 47403
www.iuniverse.com
1-800-Authors (1-800-288-4677)

Because of the dynamic nature of the Internet, any web addresses or links contained in this book may have changed since publication and may no longer be valid. The views expressed in this work are solely those of the author and do not necessarily reflect the views of the publisher, and the publisher hereby disclaims any responsibility for them.

Any people depicted in stock imagery provided by Getty Images are models, and such images are being used for illustrative purposes only. Certain stock imagery © Getty Images.

ISBN: 978-1-5320-7369-4 (sc)
ISBN: 978-1-5320-7370-0 (e)

Library of Congress Control Number: 2019904994

Print information available on the last page.

iUniverse rev. date: 05/16/2019

Contents

Chapter 1

New Beginnings

Three dogs … off lead … peaceful. Calm. Breathing in the country air. Enjoying life.

I am walking across a hayfield on a chilly, rainy November day in the Shenandoah Valley of Virginia. I have Mag, an elderly Australian shepherd and instigator; Zena, a two-year-old German shepherd, who follows Mag's lead; and Pearl, a Plott hound mix who is nine months old and my new adventure. My first foster dog.

I have read numerous books and spent more time than I should have researching dog foster care, adoption, and shelters. It sounded like something I could do. A way to give back. A way to help out with the big picture of too many dogs and cats without homes. I became obsessed with looking at all the faces of dogs throughout the country, waiting for a second, third, or even fourth chance at a good life. Senior dogs looking for a quiet place, adult dogs with good years to spend with a family, hopeful young dogs, and the adorable puppies. All shapes, sizes, and colors. Every imaginable mix of dog breeds.

Chapter 2

Walking Three

Back to the field. There is no time to daydream when out with this crew. Zena has been the baby for the last two years. I have probably kept her on a leash too long. The training manuals talk about when to trust your dog. The timing never seemed quite right. We are away from traffic and other dogs and people. But Zena got fast quickly and has long legs—four of them—for running. I have short legs—and only two—so not so much off-leash work. But now with the puppy, Zena has to be a good example—right? Right!

At the moment all three dogs are trotting up the fence line, sniffing the vole holes. Everyone is busy and happy.

Then all of a sudden the tide turns. Pearl wants to play. She jumps at Zena, barking and grabbing her on the face. Zena grabs Pearl around the neck, and then they are play fighting with growling and teeth. The chasing begins.

Chapter 3

Typical Things to Remember after a Morning Dog Walk

Don't forget to pick up the turkey bone in the front hayfield. Zena did a good "leave it," but I couldn't go pick it up or she would have thought Pearl was getting the bone.

Find my earmuffs in the back wildlife area. Zena dropped them there somewhere. I threw them as a distraction when Zena got in a frenzy.

Throw away the tissue in my jeans pocket and then wash or burn the pants. I used the tissue to remove possum poop from our trail.

Don't fall on the back porch where the water froze when I was filling the chickens' water. Puppy help makes for lots of spilling.

Right now I am enjoying the peace and quiet of three tired and full dogs sleeping together on the rug while I sip a blissful cup of white tea.

Whoops, spoke too soon. The Plott is up and looking out the window at the bird feeder. She loves to watch the birds clean up around the bird feeder and would love to chase them. And she's down again. Maybe I'll have time for a second cup after all. Hah!

Chapter 4

Pearl the Plott

Pearl the Plott came to us in the fall with the name Harriet. She had been listed on Petfinder.com and rescueme.org. She had survived negligence and the horrid puppy disease parvo. She was nine months old at the time. Through it all her tail wagged.

Pearl is finally sort of taking a nap right now, with heavy eyes watching me and blinking from time to time. I can sit down for a minute. We have been very busy since we picked up Pearl Saturday afternoon in Martinsburg, West Virginia. When we met her, she was kind of shell-shocked from a full day of riding in I don't know how many vehicles on her journey from a

southern shelter to a new home—a new chance at life. She is a tail-wagging cutie, black with brindle legs, ears, and face. Pearl was starving when we got her. Her ribs could be counted, and her hip bones and backbone were pronounced. We feed her a little at a time so she doesn't wolf down her food in one big inhale. At least this way there is some chewing involved.

So far in our journey together, Pearl has met my two dogs, Mag and Zena. We were a little leery about Zena's reaction to Pearl. Zena is very jealous of anyone who gets attention from my husband and me. Zena hasn't attempted to eat Pearl yet. They have had increasing play and walk times together. I supervise but do little intervention. Like my dog-training nephew says, the less human intervention, the better. They play hard at chasing each other.

Pearl gives as good as she gets, chewing on Zena's face and neck.

Nighttime has gone pretty well, too. Zena still sleeps in a crate in our bedroom. I put Pearl's crate right beside Zena's crate. I have only had to get up one time in the middle of the night during the first two nights. The third night Pearl slept until five o'clock in the morning and went back to bed for a little while after a short potty break.

Pearl is getting into a routine. We all go to the barn in the morning to feed cows, ponies, and the barn cat. She shows a passing interest in the other animals, as if they are new to her, but doesn't attempt to give chase.

Pearl is a delight to take into new places. She doesn't react to other dogs or people. She is friendly without jumping up on people and children she meets.

Zena, our German shepherd, had never been in a house before we brought her home. Her first smell of chicken baking in the oven got her so excited she didn't know what to do. Pearl is like that times ten! Not only is being in a house new to her, but so is food. So far we can't really eat meals in front of her. Once she knows she is always going to get her next meal, she will be able to handle others eating—we hope!

Pearl is really good about staying with us on walks. After three days she knows where the house is and where all the doors to the house are and wants to go back to them—*food in there*. She leads the way, nose to the ground, tail in the air waving back and forth like an exclamation point. The dogs take turns finding the best smells in the field.

Pearl is doing great with car riding. She is happy on the front seat driving around the farm and in her crate when we go out for coffee or to visit Tractor Supply, PetSmart, Petco, Lowes, Home Depot, and other pet-friendly stores. The puparazzi have followed Zena since she was a cute pup. Now Zena's public find Pearl the Plott the cute one and the attention-getter.

Little Pearl is taking a needed afternoon nap in the sunshine on the floor. She is settling in and getting comfortable.

On night five, Zena and Pearl finally settle in the same room after seven o'clock. Yeah! Hallelujah! But we still can't eat in front of her.

On day six, Pearl can catnap in the house instead of pacing constantly. She settles about four times for thirty minutes each nap.

After about a week of taking turns babysitting Pearl in the basement while one of us eats quickly upstairs at the counter, we can finally eat at the table in front of her. As long as Pearl can't actually see the food, and it is well away from the edge of the table, she can handle it. Progress!

I usually get ready for the day while the dogs are still in their crates in the morning. Since it was Sunday morning and my husband is an early bird, I was hoping to sleep in a bit while he took the dogs out. So when the whining started, I had to hurry out in my pj's.

Then after I had fed the dogs, I took Pearl upstairs in the bathroom with two toys so I could attempt to get my day started. Pearl played with her toys briefly and then started swinging off the end of the lace curtain, followed by chewing on a pack of toilet paper. And to think Zena used to just lie there quietly and chew on the rug.

Chapter 5

Plott Belly

Whoa! We have to cut back on your food. That Plott belly has gone from skinny to plump, Plott. And in one week!

The Plott does thicken!

Chapter 6

Shawn the Sheep

Pearl has become increasingly comfortable in her home. I have started calling her Shawn, the sheep, from Wallace and Gromit, *A Close Shave*. Like Shawn, Pearl is always chewing on something. I was housecleaning when Pearl's inner clock said *supper time*. She went from the little angel following the vacuum around to Shawn, the sheep, chewing her way into the feed room for some food!

She will chew anything—chair legs, socks (on your feet or not), a new board that was to become a cabinet, trash cans, stair treads, rugs, newel posts, my Crocs, flip-flops, the door frame … Hopefully this phase will pass quickly!

Chapter 7

What Cat?

Cat in a tree.

Cat still in a tree. Supper time. Come on, cat. We give up. Let's go in.

Chapter 8

The Journey Continues

Pearl's journey continues. As the weather warms and spring draws closer, Pearl gets more and more energized. She likes chasing flying bugs, lying sprawled out on the grass in the sunshine, and chewing on Zena, the German shepherd. She is tail wagging in her training classes—happy to be there with all her friends and her best snack, Cheerios.

Just for Fun

Chapter 9

Pearl Plays: A Conversation between Pearl and Zena

ZENA: Give up! Do you give up?

PEARL: I'll never give up!

ZENA: Give up! Give up! Do you give up?

PEARL: No, I'll never give up!

ZENA: I am a little thirsty.

PEARL: Let's get a drink.

Pearl the Plott finally gives in and trots to the water bowl. As soon as she stops drinking, Pearl grabs Zena by the face.

ZENA: I give up!

Chapter 10

The Author Has a Conversation with Her Three Dogs

"Mag, Zena, Pearl, whoever you are—*stop that.*" I don't see how people with three or more dogs keep their names straight. But maybe it's just me.

"Pearl, leave it."

"Zena, let go of Pearl's harness."

"Mag, where are you going?"

"Pearl, leave Zena's ears alone."

"Zena, would you stop!"

"Mag, come back here. Oh well, maybe I'll go with you. Where are you going?"

Chapter 11

Pearl Takes a Toy

PEARL: Sneak …

Sneak, sneak, sneak …

ZENA: I've got my eye on you!

PEARL: Sneak …

Sneak, sneak, sneak …

ZENA: That's my Kong!

PEARL: Sneak …

Sneak, sneak, sneak … Got it!

ZENA: Oh well. Who wants a toy with Plott mouth on it!

Chapter 12

Zena and Pearl Take a Walk—or Not!

"Let's walk, girls."

Oh no! The Plott plop. Pearl dropped into the grass and started wiggling back and forth with her legs wagging in the air.

Double oh no! The GSD flop. Zena also dropped to the grass and turned upside down. Pearl started chewing on Zena's harness.

"Girls, we need to walk!" I took two Cheerios out of my pocket. Both dogs hopped up, ate their Cheerios, and continued our walk down the driveway. About ten feet! Then we had another Plott plop and GSD flop. *More Cheerios!*

Epilogue

We have had Pearl for three years now. She is what is fondly called a foster failure. We adopted her shortly after we got her.

She has come a long way from the skinny, sick, little tail-wagging stray to the beautiful sweet dog that she is today. She is now an expert at welcoming new foster dogs into our home and helping teach them the skills they need to become a family dog.

I go to sleep every night listening to the soft sounds of her snoring after a happy day of working and playing with the other dogs. Pearl has found her forever home.

And for those of you who look at Pearl and say, "She's not a Plott hound," Pearl probably is a mix of Plott, Lab, and a joyful who knows what. She has become more Lab-looking as she has grown up. That's part of the fun of getting a dog who is a mix.